MANKIND IN DECLINE:
GENETIC DISASTERS, HUMAN-ANIMAL HYBRIDS, OVERPOPULATION, POLLUTION, GLOBAL WARMING, FOOD AND WATER SHORTAGES, DESERTIFICATION, POVERTY, RISING VIOLENCE, GENOCIDE, EPIDEMICS, WARS, LEADERSHIP FAILURE

STEPHEN BLAHA

MANKIND IN DECLINE:
GENETIC DISASTERS,
HUMAN-ANIMAL HYBRIDS,
OVERPOPULATION, POLLUTION, GLOBAL
WARMING, FOOD AND WATER SHORTAGES,
DESERTIFICATION, POVERTY, RISING VIOLENCE,
GENOCIDE, EPIDEMICS, WARS,
LEADERSHIP FAILURE

STEPHEN BLAHA

BLAHA RESEARCH

To My Wife Margaret

Some Other Books by Stephen Blaha

America's Future: an Islamic Surge, ISIS, al Qaeda, World Epidemics, Ukraine, Russia-China Pact, US Leadership Crisis (Blaha Research, Auburn, NH, 2014).

The Rises and Falls of Man – Destiny – 3000 AD: New Support for a Superorganism MACRO-THEORY of CIVILIZATIONS From CURRENT WORLD TRENDS and NEW Peruvian, Pre-Mayan, Mayan, Anatolian, and Early Egyptian Data, with a Projection to 3000 AD (Blaha Research, Auburn, NH, 2014).

SuperCivilizations: Civilizations as Superorganisms (McMann-Fisher Publishing, Auburn, NH, 2010).

The Rhythms of History: A Universal Theory of Civilizations (Pingree-Hill Publishing. Auburn, NH, 2002).

A Unified Quantitative Theory Of Civilizations and Societies: 9600 BC - 2100 AD (Pingree-Hill Publishing. Auburn, NH, 2004).

The Life Cycle of Civilizations (Pingree-Hill Publishing. Auburn, NH, 2002).

All the Multiverse! Starships Exploring the Endless Universes of the Cosmos using the Baryonic Force (Blaha Research, Auburn, NH, 2014)

All the Universe! Faster Than Light Tachyon Quark Starships & Particle Accelerators with the LHC as a Prototype Starship Drive Scientific Edition (Pingree-Hill Publishing, Auburn, NH, 2011).

Available on bn.com (Barnes & Noble), Amazon.com, Amazon.co.uk and other international web sites as well as at better bookstores (through Ingram Distributors).

Preface

This book discusses the ongoing and future decline in the human species. The circumstances of the decline are generally due to well-meant motives to improve the human condition. They will provide short term benefits but will result in major long term difficulties and an overall decline of the human species. Topics discussed include: The Rise of Man, Genetic Disasters, Birth Defects, Natural Changes in Human Genes, Genetic Selection for the Least Fittest, Disease/War Driven Genetic Decline, Hybrid Human-Animal Species, Social Implications of Hybrids, Religious Implications of Hybrids, Super-Human Species – Obsoleting Man, Overpopulation Constraints, Restraints on Population Growth, Achieving a Standard of Living Comparable to the United States, Population Reduction, Pollution Effects, Pollution Today and Projected for Tomorrow, Genetic Effects of Pollution, Reducing Pollution, Is Pollution Inevitable?, Global Warming, Global Temperatures over the Millenniums prior to 10,000 BC, Global Warming Today and Tomorrow, Desertification, World Deserts Today, Growth of World Deserts, Arid Earth?, Reversing Desertification, Poverty, Population and Morality, Poverty Today in Underdeveloped Countries, Poverty in Developed Countries, Political Impact of Poverty, Impact of Poverty on Population Growth, Impact of Poverty on Public Morality, Rising Violence, Violence in the Recent Past, Current Levels of Violence, Social and Political Impact of Violence, Epidemics, Past Epidemics,

Epidemics Today, Growth in Epidemic Potential with Increasing Population, Epidemics as a Method of "Culling" the Human Species, Wars, War's Effect on Population, War in the Future, Nuclear Wars are Likely, World Leadership Failure, Reduction of the Population to "Cattle", Towards a Superior Human Species?, Natural Genetic Improvements, Engineered Genetic Improvements, Cybernetic Hybrids of, and Alternatives to, Man, What of Those Left Behind?

CONTENTS

1. The Rise of Man

Species of Man have existed for at least half a million years. Modern Man has been the dominant Man-like species for the past twenty thousand years or so. Man started to ascend into large societies and civilizations about ten thousand years ago when the earth's climate began a relatively stable higher temperature period, in which we still live, although there have been relatively mild climate fluctuations. The earth's climate and environment are entering a new phase with an increasing average temperature, increasing deterioration of the environment and a major decline in the large animal species as well as massive deforestation.

In the following chapters we will analyze the impact of the changes in the earth and the changes in Man as an evolving species. Sadly the likely changes are not for the better. Instead we look to a bleaker future where the earth, Man's civilizations, and Man itself will inevitably decline if current trends continue.

Can we hope for a renewal of the earth and Man? It would seem that the chances of renewal are slim unless significant events occur. First there must be a change in the mindset of Man to a long term view to improve the environment (as opposed to the current financially driven view for exploitation of the earth's resources). Also there must be a substantial decline in the world's population to perhaps one or two billion people to reduce the overexploitation of the earth. Both of these goals would be difficult to achieve. We will discuss possibility of achieving these goals in the concluding chapters of this book.

Now we turn to an examination of the current situation of Man – painting a somewhat dismal view of the current world situation. We do this in the belief that knowing the problems will at least start us thinking more seriously of possible remedies. Ignoring problems leads to still greater problems.

The reader will be aware of many of the issues we discuss. We see the benefits of this book to be the assemblage of the major factors into an overall picture and some proposals for action to overcome major problems which the reader will find novel and provocative.

Some of the major problems that we will discuss, such as the decline in the human gene pool due to birth defect propagation, and the mitigation of Darwinian 'Survival of the Fittest' primarily by modern medicine, are not often considered in the press or books because they are distasteful or in obscure areas intellectually or geographically.

2. Genetic Disasters

Genetics rules Man. Much of what we think is based on environment is actually strongly influenced or governed by our genes although often in a subtle way. Man's set of genes are the result of a convoluted development that intertwines Man with related hominid species such as the Neanderthals and with Man's variants in different locales. It appears that modern Man originated in a small group that emerged from Africa some tens of thousands of years ago. This group with its limited gene pool enlarged its set of genes through mutations and intermixing with other Man-like species to become modern Man with a much greater variety of genes. An important part of this enlargement is the Darwinian selection rule: the survival of the fittest. Because Man dispersed into many different locales in the various continents, with small contact between the locales, region specific variants of the set of Man's genes appeared. Man became a set of "races" or groups with varying sets of genes. But Man remained one species since intermarriage between the "races" is possible and can produce fertile offspring.

In this chapter we will see the impact of aspects of modern life, and the environment, on the genetics of Man.

We suggest that the genetics of Man is in a long term decline unless major changes are made.

2.1 Birth Defects

Birth defects due to environmental and industrial pollution are on the rise worldwide in developed countries and in developing countries such as China, India and African countries. In considering birth defects beyond the sheer tragedy for its victims we have to distinguish between their short term and long term effects.

In the short term birth defects are a tragedy for individuals, their families, and their countries. A case in point is Russia, which as the former Soviet Union, created a vast amount of industrial pollution. Its effects can be seen in the rate of birth defects in newborn Russian babies: half of the newborn babies have birth defects. A human tragedy! Many of these babies will mature into adults with infirmities that will be a drain on the Russian medical system as well as their families.

If adults with birth defects marry and have children then the defects, which are typically genetic, will be passed on to future generations – perhaps leading to a larger and larger genetically defective population. Perhaps we will learn how to mitigate these genetic defects and alleviate this problem. If not then Russia will have to deal with an increasingly "disadvantaged" population.

The Russian situation is being repeated in many other countries to a greater or lesser extent. We thus must face up to a possible decline in the average genetic "health" of Man that will cause a decline in health, happiness, and prosperity over the long term.

Thus there are potential long term effects associated with birth defects caused by industrial and other forms of human pollution.

A particularly bad scenario that is not unlikely is the appearance of significant birth defects that have the side effect of promoting increased fertility, promiscuity, and sexual activity. The major possible consequence of this combination of birth defects would be the growth of an ever increasing defective part of the human population. No one know why the Neanderthals were "replaced" by humans since their physical characteristics and technology were not inferior to humans.. It is possible that a combination of gene differences including a larger human fertility rate simply drowned the Neanderthal population with a surge of human population growth. We are reminded how the American Indian tribes were swamped and driven close to extinction by an ever increasing influx of Europeans and their progeny.

The birth defects that currently dominate do not encourage a surge in defect ridden population. Typically people with birth defects have associated health problems. However the scenario posed above is not impossible. Therefore genetic research and the elimination of birth defect promoting pollution should be strongly pursued – particularly in China and India which are undergoing massive industrialization and have large populations.

2.2 Natural Changes in Human Genes

The human race is slowly evolving through genetic changes in members of the human population. The overall character of the changes is random. Some changes in individuals will lead to an increase in the segment of the population containing the genetic change. Some changes will disappear with time as the individuals with these changes die.

Generally the overall pace of change in the human race is slow and probably takes, on the average, hundreds of generations. This is evident from the past history of humanity.

Is there a distinct drift in the evolution of humanity? Is it becoming more intelligent, or less intelligent? Is it growing in size on the average or not?

Over a long time frame of the order of millions of years Man has become larger and more intelligent on average. The future evolution of Man is not so certain. The factors that led to the increase in intelligence and size of Man follow from the Darwinian selection rule of "Survival of the Fittest." Increase in intelligence and size favor survival.

If survival of the fittest were the sole selection criteria then the past trends would continue. However modern science has introduced a new factor: the use of medicine to preserve the life of infants, children and adults who in earlier times would not survive. The descendants of this population of survivors will possibly become a significant part of the population and thereby lower the average physical strength, health, and intelligence of humanity. The result might be a significant decline in the human race.

2.3 Genetic Selection for the Least Fittest

Morality, and a regard for the humane treatment of the helpless, ill and infirm, leads us to provide care and medical treatment for the less fortunate. The lack of food and potable water in many parts of the world drive the more fortunate to help.

But one must ask about the long term implications of these efforts. If we feed and clothe a child who, in the natural course of events, would not survive to adulthood, what shall we do about the adult? Should we not feed and clothe the adult as well? Can we (the world population) afford to feed and clothe large numbers of people who will continue to increase in number until the entire mass of humanity is impoverished?

Man has a problem: helping those in need can lead to a decline in Man if allowed to continue indefinitely. This path is the path to the 'least fittest' which no one could favor.

There are several potential solutions to this quandary: 1) the very harsh response of not providing any medical or sustenance to those in need; 2) a less harsh response of providing some medical assistance and sustenance on a random basis;[1] and 3) providing medical assistance and sustenance on the basis of the principle of

---

[1] This is the current practice.

'no extraordinary measures to prolong life.'[2] Thus those that have no hope of a decent life should be allowed to pass away. The judgment of what constitutes an 'extraordinary measure' is somewhat subjective and is perhaps best left to those immediately concerned with a patient.

The alternative to providing 'unlimited' care and food to those unable to live without much care is a growing population of people with low education capability, low mechanical skill capabilities, and significant health issues. Given the growth in the earth's population this alternative can only lead to global disaster.

2.4 Disease/War Driven Genetic Decline

Most genetic changes take place in small populations and either grow or decline. Major, sudden genetic changes can take place due to disease (plague) or war to the point of genocide. A disease can favor a group of individuals with a certain genetic makeup and not favor others. An example of this selectivity of diseases is the devastating effect of European diseases on native Indian populations in the Americas. Often native populations were totally decimated and replaced by Europeans of different genetic stock.

Wars leading to the elimination of peoples or to the mixing of genetic features also have major genetic consequences. An example of this type of genetic change

---

[2] This principle is favored and practiced in many hospitals. It is also favored by numerous religious groups.

is the mixing of European and native Indians in Mexico and Peru as well as other South American countries.

A more subtle genetic effect of war is the decimation of selected segments of the combatants. For example in World War I the British upper classes and the population of British poets was seriously depleted by the war.

The overall mixing of populations world-wide with differing genetic features has enabled the human race to remain one species. Otherwise humanity would have evolved into several differing species which would have severely exacerbated race relations and perhaps led to 'species wars.'

In a sense, wars, particularly large wars, do not conform to the Darwinian concept of survival of the fittest except in the case of physical strength and dexterity. Qualities of the mind are not "selected" – a bullet does not distinguish between intellectual abilities.

Thus modern man will not necessarily improve due to wars, or the primarily scientific/medical mechanisms that circumvent 'survival of the fittest.'

3. Hybrid Human-Animal Species

Creatures that were part human and part animal have been discussed since near the dawn of human civilizations – over five thousand years ago and probably much longer. In ancient Egypt many gods were composites of man and animals such as the Sphinx. In Greece creatures and gods were often part man – part animal.

Modern genetics has opened the door to the creation of creatures that combine human and animal genes. At the moment experiments involve inserting human genes within the DNA of animals. In the future true human-animal hybrids will be created. Since Man and apes are genetically quite similar it is likely that man-apes may be the first large human-animal hybrids making the underpinnings of the *Planet of the Apes* movies a reality. Other combinations of man and animals are also feasible. As the atomic bomb proved, if Man can make something he will undoubtedly make it, if some purpose motivates it. Possible purposes beyond scientific research include: making creatures to perform dangerous tasks based on the presumption that these creatures would be 'disposable,' making creatures for specialized tasks including space exploration, making creatures for sordid purposes such as 'sex slaves,' and making creatures with advanced 'superhuman' capabilities.

If such creatures are created a number of important social and religious/moral issues arise.

3.1 Social Implications

Hybrid-human creatures raise important social issues about the relation of Man and hybrids: moral questions about their use and abuse, social questions as to their role in society, and legal questions as to their rights to freedom and the protection of the law like humans. There are also the questions of black-market creation and trading in hybrids, and the use of hybrids in sex trade and hard labor. These questions have much of the tenor, and the problems, of the slavery issues of the past. Could certain types of hybrids be allowed to vote and enjoy the benefits of citizenship and the protection of the legal system? These problems would be particularly important if hybrids were endowed with intelligence comparable to Man.

For these reasons one may well ask if hybrid creation should be strictly prohibited and specialized robots developed to serve the purposes that hybrids might have served. The issues resulting from the creation of hybrids are so important that they appear to justify their prohibition.

3.2 Religious Implications of Hybrids

If hybrids are created with an intelligence comparable to Man then their place in religions becomes important. Most higher religions believe men have souls. Does an intelligent hybrid have a soul? Since there is no experimental method to prove or disprove the existence of a soul in an entity, it would not be possible to determine whether hybrids have souls. Then we would have the difficult issue of determining whether the destruction of hybrids was moral, and also the issue of whether hybrids could join religions and become priests or ministers. Could they be regarded as 'abominations' in some religions? It appears the religious status of hybrids in religions would be a totally open question. A deeper problem exists if hybrids had the general appearance and intelligence of humans. Would the similarity to Man reduce the regard for men and make it easier to treat men as a form of hybrid – thus reducing Man to an entity of lower status.

The religious implications resulting from the creation of intelligent hybrids suggest that we should create specialized robots –not hybrids – to avoid worldwide distress.

3.3 Super-Human Species – Obsoleting Man

If we can create hybrids with higher intelligence or greater strength than Man then we encounter the 'superman problem.' Ordinary men would then be at a disadvantage in obtaining work. Further there would be disturbances among workers just as there were in early 19th century England and Europe at the beginning of the Industrial Revolution.

The six billion plus people on the planet would deeply resent being placed in an inferior position to superhuman hybrids. Social disturbances would result – not just for jobs – but for the need for respect that most men desire.

The creation of superman armed forces would also be a source of major trouble and lead to more devastating wars.

Lastly the possibility exists that 'superman' hybrids, if they existed in numbers, could possibly unite and attempt to take control of governments or of the world. Then Man would become a secondary species and not the 'crowning' point of creation as many religious believe. The result would either be periodic rebellions or a catastrophic war between Man and superhuman hybrids – 'superhybrids.'

4. Overpopulation Constraints

The world population was growing slowly in the early part of the past ten thousand years. The growth rate was retarded by starvation, disease and warfare. In recent times medicine has improved to the extent that significantly more people survive diseases. The continually increase in the world food supply has supported population growth. Unwanted babies are no longer exposed in the weather to let them die. Warfare has been proportionately limited as a means of population control – we live in more peaceful times – although the future is uncertain due to the existence of weapons of mass destruction.

The net result of these 'happier' times is a rapidly increasing population that may/will soon strain the earth's resources and act as a 'natural' break on further population growth.

Currently the world population is six billion. It is projected to increase to at least nine billion by 2050. Given the current strain on the earth's resources one can only expect a further deterioration in the human condition by 2050 and beyond.

4.1 Restraints on Population Growth

Other than a major war using weapons of mass destruction or an unlikely collision with a large devastating asteroid, the major restraints on population growth are poverty, starvation, deadly pollution, and epidemics.

Recently a study[3] of epidemics appears to show that the number of epidemics has increased by a factor of four since 1980. As the population increases the number of potential sources of new epidemic diseases increases and a larger, more dense population facilitates their spread – particularly via air travel. Thus epidemics may be viewed as Nature's means of restoring stability – in this case, in the size of the population.

Epidemic diseases as well as the other mechanisms mentioned above could very likely lead to a maximum human population size. The maximum size remains to be determined. But it appears to be significantly more than nine billion. At that maximum, humanity would be in a sorry state indeed.

4.2 Achieving a Standard of Living Comparable to the United States

Having seen the restraints on population growth and being aware of the sad state to which a large population would lead, we now consider the possibility of an optimal world population which can live with a standard of living similar to that of the United States.

---

[3] K. Smith et al, Journal of the Royal Society DOI: 10.1098/rsif.2014.0950.

In Blaha (2010) we showed that the maximum size of a world population with a resource utilization rate (consumption rate) that would give the world population a standard of living at the same level as the United States is about one billion people. The calculation is based on current facts: a current world population of six billion where the United States consumes 40% of the world's production while having only about 5% of the world's population.

World production for six billion people would have to increase by a factor of roughly 8 for the average world standard of living to be that of the US: eight times more food, eight times more housing, eight times more industry, and so on. Clearly, this is an impossible task for the earth to achieve and sustain.

To achieve a U.S. standard of living with current world production, the world population should be approximately equal to the U.S. population of 300 million plus the ratio of remaining world production to production devoted to the US (0.6/0.4) times 300 million.[4] The total population would then have to be 750 million people. The world population would have to be very much smaller if everybody was to live at the U.S. standard of living. There is no hope for a U.S. level of standard of living for the current or projected world population.

When we consider the pollution, constrained food production, and energy and global warming problems as

---

[4] This additional term takes account of using the remaining world production (60% of total world production) to support a population at the U.S. standard of living.

well as the pollution of the oceans then it is clear that we cannot increase world production without major difficulties. It is also clear that a stable world would undoubtedly require an approximately equal standard of living for all. Therefore the population of the world must be significantly reduced, or it must tolerate major inequalities in the standard of living of various regions and nations.

4.3 Population Reduction

The problem of reducing the world's population is a major problem that leads to major social and religious difficulties. It also opens the question of how to accomplish the reduction: by nation, by ethnicity, by religious affiliation, and so on? There are also more subtle issues such as the possible reduction of the human gene pool and the disappearance of certain ethnic groups such as small tribes of primitive peoples.

These problems would seem to make major population reduction an impossible task. It also raises the question of whether such an attempt should be made. Perhaps a world with a large population and a clear policy of pollution control and cleanup would be more desirable. Possibly natural or man-made events will lead to a sharp reduction in population. The proper approach is thus unclear.

China is making an attempt to reduce its population. It is clearly very unpopular with its people and suggests only a totalitarian state could succeed in population reduction with the Chinese approach.

India has tentative, voluntary programs supporting population reduction. However there is a large segment of the Indian population who wish to have children that will support them in their old age. Thus there is popular opposition to population limitation.

European countries, and the United States, are in native population reduction. The primary cause of this phenomenon appears to be the expense of having children and the 'poor' future their children would appear to have.

Africa and the Islamic people of the Mideast are in the midst of a population boom favored by native customs and their religious views.

Based on these considerations the only possible ways to reduce the population are epidemics/plagues, nuclear war, and a massive natural catastrophe. These possibilities are not appealing. Neither is a poverty-stricken, starving, pollution-ridden world.

5. Pollution

Pollution is a much talked about phenomenon. We see it on land, in the air, and now in the oceans. We know its origin – us. We know that the elimination of most pollution is an expensive and time consuming process.

A consideration that has not been addressed as far as this author knows is the possibility that pollution is a necessary part of human activity and may be unavoidable. If this view is correct then the question arises whether the value of human production is more or less than the cost of pollution cleanup. If pollution cleanup is more costly then Man will inexorably cause a decline in the earth's ability to support human civilizations, and there will be a continuous, perhaps slow, decline in Man caused by the decline in the environment.

In this chapter we will overview the pollution situation and its effects, consider pollution cleanup, and lastly consider whether increasing pollution is inevitable or avoidable.

5.1 Pollution Today and Projected for Tomorrow

Sadly, no one has studied the relation between world population and *total* world pollution to the author's knowledge. The calculation of total world pollution is a difficult one due to the varied nature and dispersal of pollutants around the world. A major issue is how to sum the various pollutants. How does one add the mercury pollution in the world's oceans to the waste in toxic dumps in a meaningful way? It is clearly not simple addition.

Perhaps the best method to calculate total world pollution – component by component – is to calculate the cost to clean up each pollutant component. How much would it cost to lower ocean mercury levels to an acceptable value? How much would it cost to clean up all toxic dumps? How much would it cost to neutralize all the world's garbage piles and dumps? How much would it cost to clean up the 25% of the world's farmland that is polluted? The sum of these numbers plus other pollutant cleanup numbers would produce a meaningful estimate of world pollution in financial terms. It would also give world planners a means of determining whether the world is improving or deteriorating? The author believes it would show an ever increasing pollution level – particularly in view of the increase in the price of gold that will undoubtedly increase ocean mercury levels.[5]

A study of the rate of the increase in pollution levels is necessary for effective planning for the future. It could also influence Man's activities in such a way as to reduce the rate of pollution increase.

---

[5] The rapid growth in Chinese industry and consequent pollution is clearly another reason to believe the world pollution rate is increasing. The use of poisonous metals in computer hardware, and the growing computer hardware industry, is also promoting pollution rate growth.

5.2 Effects of Pollution

The effects of pollution are all too evident: increasing rates of birth defects, increasing incidence of cancer particularly in children and in mature women, increasing educational problems of youth such as dyslexia caused by low levels of toxicity in land and water, and increased medical problems for all ages of people caused by toxic waste and befouled food and water.

The net result of these pollution induced problems is personal and family tragedies, and large medical and personal expenses.

5.3 Reducing Pollution

The long term reduction of pollution is going to be a long, tedious and expensive process. It will be more feasible in advanced countries which have the resources to reduce existing pollution. It will be more difficult for developing countries because they lack the financial ability for toxic waste cleanup, and because their efforts to grow lead them to increase environmental pollution to lower production costs for their products. China is the notorious example of this second problem.

The form of pollution reduction for soil on a large scale will probably require either chemicals or bacteria that will effectively neutralize toxic ingredients. Hopelessly polluted land, such as radioactively contaminated land, could be buried in deep mines. Water purification or decontamination can be accomplished through neutralizing chemicals or through bacteria that concentrate and neutralize the contaminants.

The best approach to preventing pollution is to develop new packaging methods that rapidly degrade to harmless material after use. Methods of manufacturing, mining and farming could also be changed to be far less polluting. These efforts will require a major chemical industry effort to find non-polluting alternatives.

5.4 Is Pollution Inevitable?

Pollution can be sharply reduced by the use of non-polluting or pollution reduction techniques. However the production of waste by industry and people will undoubtedly continue. Waste can be made non-polluting, so the disposal of non-polluting waste materials is not of great consequence. It could be used to build islands and extend land into the sea. It could also be used to fill old expended mines. There are also vast areas of unusable desert land or chains of mountains (such as the Rocky mountains) that can be filled with neutralized waste. Waste due to human endeavor is inevitable but pollution can be largely reduced or eliminated.

Without a concerted effort to reduce the amount of pollution Man will change to a much less successful species.

6. Global Warming

It has become increasingly clear that the average temperature of the earth is slowly increasing. The increase is causing climactic changes in various regions of the earth. As the earth's temperature increases more changes can be expected that will benefit some regions and be to the detriment of other regions.

6.1 Global Temperatures over the Millenniums prior to 10,000 BC

Before 10,000 years ago there were major fluctuations in the earth's temperature and Man was largely composed of hunter-gatherer groups. For unknown reasons the temperature of the earth then stabilized at a relatively high level that has remained the same since then except for relatively small fluctuations. Since the stabilization began, human societies and civilizations have developed.

6.2 Global Warming Today and Tomorrow

Recently, in the past one hundred years or so the average earth temperature has begun to rise leading to climactic changes that promise to lead to warmer northern and southern regions near the earth's poles. The warming of the polar regions has resulted in the melting of ice and glaciers that will soon lead to rising sea levels that will inundate coastal regions around the world.

On the positive side global warming will facilitate food production in northern Canada, Siberia, and northern Scandinavia as well as the southern tip of South America. The great area of these regions will enable a large increase in the world's food supply. The longer days in polar regions are very beneficial for crop production despite the shorter growing season. Anyone who has seen the 'giant' vegetables produced in Alaska can appreciate the potential of the polar regions for crop production.

7. Desertification

7.1 World Deserts Today

The earth's deserts today cover a substantial area. The major deserts are primarily in tropical regions such as the Sahara, a band of desert stretching into China and the Gobi desert, and so on. There is also a band of desert around the north polar regions. About one-third of the earth's land area is desert.

The future of Man is intimately associated with the amount of land available for food production. And so the preservation of arable soil with sufficient rainfall is of great importance.

Unfortunately the earth's deserts are growing. A major cause of the growth of deserts is overgrazing and farming in the marginal areas at the borders of deserts. This effect is clearly evident in Africa and may become an issue if North American drought areas continue to lack sufficient rainfall.

Changes in weather – growing droughts in certain areas – are also causing the growth of deserts. An extreme example of this phenomenon – the loss of water supply – is now being blamed for the demise of the first Chinese kingdom, Hongshan,[6] 6,500 years ago. A severe drought caused the kingdom to rapidly change to desert in a few years. The population dispersed to other parts of China – with the indirect benefit of spreading Chinese civilization.

7.2 Growth of World Deserts

The growth of the world's deserts is a cause of great concern. Much of it is due to overgrazing in regions near deserts with marginal rainfall.

There is also a long term problem – the overuse of underground water supplies that will not be replenished very soon. Underground water supplies are being rapidly depleted in California and in other regions. When these water supplies are exhausted the farmlands dependent on them will revert to desert thus reducing food supplies.

Other regions ripe for desertification include:

Africa
China
Central Asia
South America
Other parts of the U.S.

7.3 Arid Earth?

Given the potential for the growth of deserts and the impact on the world food supply, it is reasonable to consider the possibility of a semi-arid earth. The consequences would be enormous – mass starvation of the human race – perhaps spread over a period of

---

[6] Hongshan was located in northern China several millennia before the first historically known Chinese kingdoms.

hundreds of years. Under extreme conditions it would seem reasonable to create a network of aqueducts that would transport water to arid regions. This network could be fed by natural water supplies as well as the use of massive desalination plants to recycle ocean water to fresh water. The plants could be powered by nuclear or fusion energy, should fusion energy become a reality.

7.4 Reversing Desertification

The reversal of desertification is possible. This has been proven on a small scale in Israel and Egypt through very economical direct watering of trees one by one.

It could also be implemented by the planting of trees and bushes (as is being done in China and other countries) to prevent wind erosion and to utilize the trees and bushes as mini reservoirs.

Sewer sludge can be used to stabilize soil and fertilize the growth of plants.

Lastly, the development of large fusion powered efficient energy could lead to major efforts to produce fresh water from ocean water.

7.5 Decline or Not?

There is a contest between the growth of arable land through the global warming of polar regions, and the decline of arable land due to higher ocean levels and desertification. This contest will be part of the determination whether Man will grow or decline as a species.

8. Poverty, Population and Morality

8.1 Poverty Today in Underdeveloped Countries

In many underdeveloped countries, and in some developed countries, there are pockets of poverty and starving people. These problem areas exist because the distribution of food and wealth in the world is not uniform.

Sufficient food could be provided to all of the world's people. However in so providing food to all, the economics of farming would be severely affected, and the difficult question of who should pay for the food – individual governments or a United Nations agency funded by the member governments – would be difficult to settle.

Thus poverty, and particularly food shortages, are the result of political and economic considerations.

8.2 Poverty in Developed Countries

There are pockets of poverty and starvation in developed countries. The problem is similar to that described in section 8.1. The economics and politics of a national food program to alleviate the suffering of the poor, and to particularly ensure every child has a sufficient diet, are difficult to arrange in such a way as to avoid economic difficulties for farmers and to avoid corrupt practices and unfair distribution of food.

Those who may feel that a better food distribution system for the poor is not needed in countries such as the United States should consider that one in every thirty children is homeless, and many families are homeless as well. These people do not have access to government food programs and their only recourse is to overburdened private shelters and food banks.

Given the large number of unemployed and underemployed people in the United States and other countries, and given their general lack of employable skills, the plight of the poor will not easily or quickly be remedied. Government job programs exist. But reality suggests that some will never be employable despite having the ability to work and their lack of physical disabilities. In this case a subsidy program would be appropriate if it could be crafted to avoid misuse.

8.3 Political Impact of Poverty

The political impact of poverty on a nation, and thereby the world, is to promote the growth of the bad instincts of the world's peoples. Where there should be peace and prosperity, the people of the world's nations degenerate to unsavory business practices, lying, cheating, stealing and greed. The spread of these vices eventually leads to civil unrest and wars.

Attempts to alleviate the problems of poverty can lead to 'bread and circuses' societies that, like Rome, led to social and political decay.

8.4 Impact of Poverty on Population Growth

The impact of poverty, and a tight economy, on Man's population growth is quite evident. It can be seen in the countries of Europe and now in the United States. The native populations of these countries have declining birth rates and a stable or declining population.

The reason for the population situation of developed countries is the feeling of the people that they cannot, and prefer not, to have children if they cannot support them adequately. There is also a feeling that the future of these countries is not promising for their children. The classic American feeling that life will be better for their children is no longer widely believed.

In many underdeveloped countries people feel that having children is beneficial because their children will support them in their old age. Consequently the population of underdeveloped countries is generally increasing. To some extent this increase is due to the current availability of food at a relatively cheap price.

The net effect of the combination of decreasing developed country populations and increasing undeveloped country populations is to increase the relative proportion of less educated, poorer people in humanity.

Over a long period of time, if this situation persists, Man will degenerate into a lower educated, poverty ridden populace. The result: a rather grim future.

8.5 Impact of Poverty on Public Morality

Poverty has many effects that influence society in the short and long term. One effect that is becoming increasingly evident – particularly in developed countries such as the United States – is a growth in crime and violence. The tight finances of the American middle class, and the seemingly inescapable cycle of poverty of the poor and lower middle classes have led to increasing crime: shop lifting, theft, robberies, burglaries, and so on.

Family life is suffering due to financial problems. Homelessness of families – *and children* – has increased significantly. Financial problems have increased marital breakups and counteracted attempts to increase the educational level of children. Poor, hungry, children from homes in discord cannot become educational achievers.

In addition to the above issues the growing financial problems of the middle class (Pay is not increasing nearly as fast as the cost of living.) have led to a decline in morality – growth in prostitution and other sex crimes, and a breakdown of respect for the law. We can see that effect in the increasing attacks on policemen and the increasing tendency for looting and rioting. It is not uncommon for looters to help provoke riots so that they can pursue looting with the police distracted by riots.

We conclude that an increasing poorer world will lead Man to an uneducated, immoral, disturbed level with a consequent breakdown of social order and civilization.

9. Rising Violence

9.1 Violence in the Recent Past

The amount of violence in the past – from fifty to one hundred years ago – was more or less proportional to the population. In the West it was fairly closely correlated with the proportion of the population living in poverty or at the level of lower middle class income.

Generally violence had three components: criminally insane people acting their psychoses, persons seeking revenge for real or imagined wrongs, and individuals who were primarily interested in financial gain.

9.2 Current Levels of Violence

Recently violence has added new dimensions: terrorism to achieve political/social goals, much greater crime by newly homeless people in developed countries, theft of homes and property using intimidation by the newly homeless, major growth in scams and fraud, major growth in theft in stores and government facilities such as post offices and customs inspections, increasing murders of government officials and policemen, and major disrespect for the law.

Crime levels in some areas have reached the point where the police are not arresting criminals for petty crimes. There is a marked deterioration in the stability and security of western developed countries in particular.

9.3 Social and Political Impact of Violence

The social and political impact of the increasing violence will be a fragmentation of society and a decline in the national unity of Western nations. As a result the ability of the population in these countries to work together to resolve problems and defend their country will decline.

If social disorder in the West deteriorates further then Western civilization, the leading civilization of Man, will decline and will cause a decline in the advancement of Man into the future.

10. Epidemics

10.1 Past Epidemics

Past epidemics have had a major impact on the history of Man. Some of their noteworthy effects are: the defeat of the Athenians by the Spartan league in the Peloponnesian War, a major defeat of the Roman Empire leading to its fall, and the Black Death Plague of the Middle Ages which caused the death of one-quarter of the population of Europe and took two hundred years for Europe to revive. These epidemics, which are but a fraction of the epidemics afflicting the world over the course of history, illustrate the major impact of epidemics on the history of Man.

10.2 Epidemics Today

Today we are faced with a number of potential epidemics. The epidemics of recent years have not had a major impact – partly because of improved medical care and sanitary procedures.

If a major war does not break out that does not lead to a breakdown in the unified world effort to control and prevent the spread of epidemics, then there is hope that a major epidemic will not break out except under extraordinary circumstances.

Presently the only potentially dangerous epidemic in progress is Ebola. While Ebola is not yet under control, its advance has been limited to a few countries. It has been effectively eradicated in some of the infected countries. The current containment of Ebola is largely due to a major international effort.

10.3 Growth in Epidemic Potential with Increasing Population

As we described earlier a new study[7] of epidemics appears to show that the number of epidemics has increased by a factor of four since 1980.

As the world population increases the number of potential sources of new epidemic diseases increases.

A larger, denser population facilitates the emergence and spread of epidemic diseases.

The spread of epidemics has been enhanced by the use of new methods of transportation. Air travel, in particular, has become an important mechanism for the rapid spread of epidemics.

There also appears to be a new mechanism for the generation of epidemic diseases – the generation of epidemic diseases by transfer from animals to Man. Ebola is an example of this phenomenon. Ebola was first given to Man by transfer from ape and other 'bush' meat. Ebola also appears to have a reservoir in bats. It has been suggested that a certain bat-infested tree in Africa was the original source of Ebola.

---

[7] K. Smith et al, Journal of the Royal Society DOI: 10.1098/rsif.2014.0950.

10.4 Epidemics as a Method of "Culling" the Human Species

Nature seems to have mechanisms to restore balance. Excesses in natural events in one direction are compensated by natural measures that restore a balance.

A simple example of Nature's balancing act is the interplay between wolf and rabbit populations. As a rabbit population increases, the predator wolf population increases due to the larger food supply. Then as the rabbit food supply is consumed, the wolf population undergoes starvation and is reduced. Fewer wolves leads to an increase in the survivability of rabbits who then undergo population growth. Then the wolf population has more food to grow again. Thus a balance is achieved between the rabbit and wolf populations with oscillations around the balance point.

10.4.1 Balancing Act for the Human Population

Man does not have a strong predator to keep the human population in balance. And as we produce more food on more land using better fertilization techniques and improved crop strains, we see Man's population continually increasing – at least up to the present.

The only balancing possibilities are epidemics and wars. We have seen the population reducing effects of major plagues such as the Black Death. Thus epidemics may be viewed as one of Nature's means of restoring population stability. The growth in the number of epidemics since 1980 as noted above suggests that epidemics do participate in Nature's balancing act for

Man's population. This mechanism is disturbing but Nature is not exemplified by kindness if one considers the cycle of life and death in oceans, jungles and forests.

If our view of the role of epidemics is correct then we can foresee increasing numbers of severe epidemics as long as Man's population continues to increase. Our only recourse is improved medical treatment to counteract epidemics. This effort is underway now for Ebola at the Center for Disease Control and other research centers.

10.4.2 Epidemics as a 'Culling' Mechanism

Epidemics are viewed with fear and anguish. They kill people. However from the viewpoint of Darwinian 'Survival of the Fittest' epidemics serve to 'cull' the weaker elements of populations. Thus in a sense epidemics 'strengthen' the physical strength of the human race. However, since they don't select on the basis of intelligence or other positive characteristics of humanity, epidemics cannot be viewed as a mechanism for the improvement of Man. Disease does not respect the greatness in men.

The other 'population control' mechanism is war – discussed in the next chapter. It also is no respecter of human qualities.

11. Wars

In Blaha (2010) we considered the benefits and horrors of war. Below is a extract from that book that sets the stage for our subsequent discussion.

15.1.1 The Benefits of War

Mankind has cried for Peace since the beginning of recorded history. It appears in the Bible. It appears in other works such as *The Contest Between Homer and Hesiod*, which was written probably towards the end of the 2nd century (after Hadrian). In the contest, judged by King Paneides and leading Chalcidians, Homer proves the better poet but the king awards the prize to Hesiod saying that the arts of Peace (such as described in Hesiod's *Works and Days*) should transcend the Arts of War. "it was right that he who called upon men to follow peace and husbandry should have the prize rather than one who dwelt on war and slaughter."[8]

The longing for Peace reaches down to the present day. Yet throughout human history wars occur frequently. Why, one may ask, should war be so prevalent? What evolutionary advantage does it confer on Mankind that makes it a common occurrence throughout history?

In this subsection we will list some of the benefits of warfare mindful of the tremendous price that these benefits cost. In the following subsection we will describe the costs. It appears, at least in the early stages of Mankind's evolution,

---

[8] Hesiod (1982) p. 587.

waging war had an evolutionary advantage. Today's world, especially the more advanced parts, is largely the result of the technological revolution started in World War II (and to a lesser degree in World War I) and stimulated by the Cold War that followed.

Some of the major advantages of war are:

1. Darwinian Survival of the Fittest – war tends to weed out the less physically fit and less intelligent individuals and groups.
2. War plays an important role in insuring the unity of the human race by mixing peoples together in relatively large numbers. Otherwise humanity would have split into separate species. If members of different species mate they do not produce fertile offspring. (The classic example is mules: the result of mating horses and donkeys.) Some scientists have stated that if the European exploration and expansion throughout the world had not happened then possibly humanity may have separated into two species over the next two or three thousand years.
3. War is a mechanism for population control. Although it is cruel, it is clear that regions subject to constant warfare often do not experience the population growth of more peaceful regions. The Mongols frequently practiced the systematic slaughter of conquered nations and decimated the populations of some regions.
4. War, more recently, has stimulated the development of technology – especially in the 20th century – the bloodiest century in humanity's history according to Sorokin.[9] Some of the technology initiated in World War II and advanced further in the Cold War that followed are:

---

[9] Sorokin (1957).

- Electronics – major developments including radar, radios/television, miniaturization, and so on.
- Transportation: advances in ground transportation, airplanes, helicopters, jets and rocketry.
- Computers: initially mechanical, then vacuum tube based, and now transistorized. Computers are used for numerous purposes.
- Atomic energy: first developed in WW II they are increasingly used s an energy source. Nuclear radiation is used in medical applications.
- Communications: Radio, Television, and other media such as the Internet have revolutionized the world and created the "Global Village."

These technologies are the core of present-day life in the advanced part of the world. Ultimately they originated in wartime research and were developed under the stimulus of the Cold War. Since then they have become an integral part of modern life.

15.1.2 The Horrors of War

Seldom does one see that benefits of a human activity can also be its drawbacks. War has this dubious distinction. For all the listed benefits there are associated negative aspects and results. Weighing the positives and negatives of the benefits yields a net overall positive benefit.

However the negatives of war confirm the feelings of the broad majority of humanity that war is to be avoided where possible.

Some of the horrors of war are:

1. Horrible slaughters of combatants and civilians.

2. Enormous waste of natural resources.
3. Wholesale destruction of the growth previously achieved in peacetime.
4. The deaths of potential leaders of Mankind's progress in the Arts & Sciences into the future.
5. The creation of the groundwork for future wars.
6. Technical advances that are disadvantages from a societal viewpoint: improvements in torture methods, more efficient mass killing technology, bio-warfare, and so on.

Despite these horrors men will war. And prepare for war. The remainder of this chapter will be devoted to a theory of arms races, and war and peace We will start by showing the Richardson[10] theory of arms races and war uses the same dynamical equations as our energetics/thermodynamics growth theory of civilizations and our Societal Level extension of the growth theory based on a Newtonian force model. Given the impact of war on civilizations the similarity of Richardson's theory to our theory of civilizations tends to support our approach to the dynamics of civilizations. In addition the development of our cyclic civilization theory when applied to develop Richardson's equations leads to new insights into arms races such as a cyclic form of arms races and the possibility that arms races can lead to the bankruptcy of one of the players.

11.1 War's Effect on Population

It is easy to see that war causes a population to decrease through battles, the death of non-combatants, and starvation. History has witnessed many wars amongst the various branches of Man. Sorokin(1957) studied the impact of war on population and found that the 20th

---

[10] Richardson (1960) and earlier work cited therein dating back to the 1930s.

century was the bloodiest century[11] since the beginning of human history.

The additional carnage of the 20th century can be attributed to improved weaponry and technology, the broader scope of warfare due to improved transportation, and the wholesale slaughter of non-combatants partly due to ideological reasons (For example: the Russian communist slaughter of peasants by starvation after World War I), and partly because non-combatants were often used in weapons and food production to support war efforts.

War clearly reduces populations. In the past populations were often restored after hostilities ended. There are exceptions. For example, the destruction of the intricate irrigation system of Iraq by the Mongols was never remedied. Consequently the Iraqi population did not increase very quickly after the Mongols. And Iraq remained a much poorer agricultural region afterwards up to nearly the present.

The fate of culture and knowledge after warfare is usually not good. The classic examples of this effect is the burning of the Library of Alexandria and the destruction of the almost modern research efforts underway under its umbrella; the killing of Archimedes, one of the greatest scientists of antiquity, by a Roman soldier in the siege of Syracuse was another instance of decline due to war.

---

[11] Note Sorokin's study extends to 1957 and does not take account of the wars and conflicts since then that could only increase the calamity of war in the 20th century.

War has proved bad for the future of Man by killing the best and bravest of men, and promoting cultural decline.

11.2 War in the Future

War in the future can only be viewed with horror: massive death and destruction, and the possibility of a long lasting catastrophic agony for humankind.

In addition to the horrors so well introduced in the murderous 20th century we now can expect new forms of warfare: biological warfare, deadly gas warfare, improved conventional warfare using drones and other new technology, nuclear warfare, and terrorist warfare designed to frighten and destabilize societies.[12]

It is not necessary to go into the details of emerging modern warfare. One need only say that it poses grim portents for the future of Man.

11.3 Nuclear Wars are Likely

Modern weaponry such as nuclear and biological weapons bring a new dimension to warfare. In the past when a war ended, death ends – at least for the most part.

---

[12] A current example of the power of terrorists to intimidate people may be the conspicuous absence of American leaders: the President, Vice-President, the Secretary of State, prominent Presidential candidates and members of Congress to attend the 'million man march' in Paris to protest the recent terrorist attacks in France, OR EVEN TO DO MORE THAN BRIEFLY COMMENT ON THE EVENTS IF AT ALL. Compare this weak behavior to the bravery of past American leaders in more perilous times. American leaders are afraid to even speak of terrorists! It is evident to our friends and to our foes.

But nuclear and biological weapons have long term effects. One need only look at the results of the nuclear attacks on Japan in World War II and the devastating residual killing radiation from Chernobyl that is still killing and will continue to do so in the children of the future — leukemia, other cancers and so on.

The long term effect of nuclear and other new weapons will have a profound effect on the evolution of Man and could lead to the demise of Man under certain circumstances.

Where are the leaders that will bring an end to this sword of Damocles hanging over the head of Man? Or are we condemned to a future leadership produced by plastic surgery mouthing sweet words signifying nothing?

12. World Leadership Failure

Historians have often noted that some societies with small populations have extraordinary leadership. One thinks here of fifth century BC Athens, the pre-empire Roman Republic, the Founding Fathers of the United States, and so on.

Societies with large populations often have mediocre or bad leadership.

How can we understand this phenomenon? One would naturally expect that societies with large populations would have a larger pool of potential good leaders and the fierce selection process of determining the leadership would result in more outstanding leaders than small societies.

It appears, to this author, that this anomaly can be understood as due to three features of large societies: 1) the large number of individuals striving for leadership roles, and the lack of knowledge of the qualities of potential leaders in the general populace, allows misjudgments that lead to poor choices of leaders; 2) factions (political parties) often develop within large populations that can force the choice of the leaders through a snowball effect; and 3) corrupt groups that often develop in large populations can simply buy the "election" of their choice of leaders for financial gain.

A particularly clear example of the third factor is the powerful media effect on elections in the United States. Access to media advertising is strictly a matter of finances.

The second factor is evidenced by the power of ethnic groups to sway votes to leaders of their choice.

12.1 Reduction of the Population to "Cattle"

Alfred Hitchcock, the movie director, described actors as "cattle." To some extent it is reasonable to describe the people of a nation as cattle: swayed by the media, led to a consensus by discussions with 'leaders' representing political parties, and marched to a slaughter at the polling booths.

The major cause of the 'cattle effect' is the vastness of populations in large countries. Candidates for public office can have media images created for them by political advisors. These well-crafted images are designed to convince voters to vote for candidates.

Increasingly, political parties in major countries are being nudged to cater to the people by providing more government support for medical care, social benefits and increasingly for food as food prices rise. President Kennedy shows the change in America when we remember his Inauguration speech statement, "Ask not what your country can do for you, ask what you can do for your country."

Now America, and many other major countries, have aging populations who need help to live comfortably. This group is largely placid, and wishes for security and safety. They want government support knowing that they have a limited ability to earn money in an ever-inflating economy. Their goal is to receive and not to give – knowing that their earning power is weak.

The poor people in the major countries face similar problems and have a similar attitude: the government owes me!

The combined effect is a tendency to a type of socialistic government and a strong tendency to support leaders who will give them 'bread.'

The result is a world where Man is beginning to become used to living on the dole and not inclined to new ventures on earth or in space. We see Man as moving towards a static socialistic society that may end Man's future growth possibilities.

Thus Man is tending towards becoming a cattle herd – superficially led by carbon copy leaders – all with the goal of pacifying the masses. At present some nations are striving for improvement – Russia, China, and India – in particular. But their progress is driven by aggressive tendencies. If they succeed in becoming like the West they will encounter the same problems.

How can Man escape a future with a static society? It appears that the only reasonable solution is to have an optimal distribution of young, middle aged, and older people that can provide the economic and social conditions for a stable growing society. Discovering the required distribution and achieving it in a democratic manner is a difficult problem that is not yet solved. One apparent requirement is a smaller world population of the order of a billion people at most.

13. Towards a Superior Human Species?

The 6[13]th century Greek poet Hesiod[13] wrote of the five generations or races of Man: the Golden race who lived like gods without sorrow, toil, aging or wrongdoing; then the Silver race who lived as children for a hundred years and engaged in sinning and wrongdoing; then the brazen (bronze) race who were terrible, strong and fond of war; and then a god-like race of noble heroes (the heroes of the *Iliad*) who Zeus eventually placed in a paradise at the ends of the earth. The fifth generation of men – the iron race – is the race of men of the present age doomed to sorrow, toil, and grief with no help against evil.

There is an element of truth in this myth. It accurately depicts the present age of Man. Knowing that primitive Man had more leisure – a 'better' lifestyle – than the present generation of Man we see that there is a resemblance to the generation of the Golden race.

But Darwinian evolution reveals that modern Man emerged from a primitive primate species. The present state of Man is mixed. Some men live well; the majority of

---

[13] In his poem *Works and Days* translated in Hesiod (1982).

men live in a manner not different from Hesiod's depiction of the iron generation.

Why have we described Hesiod's view of the generations of Man. First, because it reveals that change in Man is not a new concept. Secondly, because it shows that Man has not changed much from the time of Hesiod. In fact it appears that Man is relatively unchanged during the length of recorded history.

A little known book, *Cosmic Consciousness*,[14] by Dr. Richard M. Bucke suggests that Man is undergoing a change for the better by considering the increase in the number of great men in the past two millennia. Whether this analysis is correct or not, it is reasonable to believe that Man will continue to evolve over a long time scale measured in hundreds of thousands of years. Where Man is a million years from now is difficult to estimate. There are genetic factors, factors dependent on history (nuclear wars?), climactic effects, and the possibility of encounters with aliens.

In this chapter we will consider some of the possible mechanisms by which Man will evolve.

13.1 Natural Genetic Improvements

Recently geneticists have developed an understanding of random genetic changes that naturally occur in nature. These changes appear to be due to the chemistry of the local environment of entities. Human genetic changes have been tracked and have been used in

---

[14] Bucke(1901). Dr. Bucke's little remembered book was acclaimed by William James and P. D. Oospensky.

the study of the migrations and interplay of human groups.

Naturally occurring changes in humans are infrequent and so humanity is changing at a slow pace. If a major external event occurred such as a plague it is conceivable that a large segment of a population would die leaving only a group, having a genetic feature(s), that protects them from the plague. Such an event has not happened in recorded history to the best of our knowledge.

Thus we find that Man is slowly changing due to 'natural causes' in various parts of the human species that will combine to produce future Man.

13.2 Engineered Genetic Improvements

Currently research, and clinical, methods are being used to repair damaged genes in individuals.

As we learn more of the genetic structure of Man it will become possible to engineer new features in Man such as improved health and greater intelligence.

The ability to change the characteristics of Man is fraught with hope and danger. We can hope to make improvements in Man to prevent major diseases and infirmities. We can make improvements in Man to prolong life and delay aging effects. We can improve the processing ability of the human mind.

Each of the listed 'improvements' above has an associated negative. Preventing diseases and infirmities lowers the demands on the human immune system that might reduce its strength. It also prevents natural selection via 'survival of the fittest.'

Prolonging life and delaying aging would change the social balance inherent in humanity. The result could be a population dominated by the aged resulting in a static society that does not have dynamic growth capabilities.

Improving the processing ability of the human mind could lead to a society where everybody wishes to do intellectual activity to the detriment of the manual activities that are essential for a functioning society. The tendency of parents and children to 'get into' white collar positions, which is evident today, would only be worsened.

Thus genetic 'improvements' in Man require careful consideration of both their short term and long term effects.

13.3 Cybernetic Hybrids of, and Alternatives to, Man

The advances in nanotechnology and computers raise the possibility of creating artificial parts to repair medical problems in people. Procedures of this sort are already being performed.

It is easy to envision the extension of human parts replacement throughout the human body.

A particularly troublesome possibility is the preservation of humans by the implantation of their brains in either human or mechanical bodies. Should this possibility be realized then enormous social and religious problems would arise. However, given the rule, 'If it is possible and financially rewarding, it will happen,' brain implantation is a serious possibility.

New computer technology can also possibly create robots with human-like features and intelligence. Such robots would be able to compete with Man and lead to the possibility of serious conflicts as well as moral/ethical issues that would challenge Man's religions.

Many of these possibilities have been the subject of science fiction movies, books and television. For this reason it seems unnecessary to discuss these possibilities in detail.

13.4 What of Those Left Behind?

Christ said, "The poor we have always with us." Whether one is religious, or not, Christ's statement reveals a truth about the human condition: the disparity in wealth in Man (due to the range of human abilities and talents) will continue into the future.

If any of the possibilities described above materialize then Man might become divided into two or more parts with different capabilities and potential for success. Divergences of this sort can be expected to lead to major conflicts based on Man's history.

One cannot stop progress but one can hope that the future will avoid difficulties as much as possible.

REFERENCES

Bernal, J. D. 1929. *The World, the Flesh and the Devil.* Indiana University Press. Bloomington, IN.

Blaha, S. 2002a. *The Rhythms of History: A Universal Theory of Civilizations.* Pingree-Hill Publishing. Auburn, NH.

_____. 2002b. *The Life Cycle of Civilizations.* Pingree-Hill Publishing. Auburn, NH.

_____. 2004a. *A Unified Quantitative Theory Of Civilizations and Societies: 9600 BC - 2100 AD.* Pingree-Hill Publishing. Auburn, NH.

_____. 2004b. *Quantum Big Bang Cosmology: Complex Space-time General Relativity, Quantum Coordinates, Dodecahedral Universe, Inflation, and New Spin 0, ½, 1 & 2 Tachyons & Imagyons.* Pingree-Hill Publishing. Auburn, NH.

_____. 2008. *A Complete Derivation of the Form of the Standard Model With a New Method to Generate Particle Masses: Second Edition.* Pingree-Hill Publishing. Auburn, NH.

_____. 2009a. *Bright Stars, Bright Universe: Advancing Civilization by Colonization Of The Solar System And The Stars Using A Fast Quark Drive.* Pingree-Hill Publishing. Auburn, NH.

_____. 2009b. *To Far Stars and Galaxies: Second Edition of Bright Stars, Bright Universe.* Pingree-Hill Publishing. Auburn, NH.

_____. 2010. *SuperCivilizations: Civilizations as Superorganisms.* McMann-Fisher Publishing, Auburn, NH.

_____, 2011b. *All the Universe! Faster Than Light Tachyon Quark Starships & Particle Accelerators with the LHC as a Prototype Starship Drive Scientific Edition.* Pingree-Hill Publishing, Auburn, NH, 2011.

_____, 2013a. *Multi-Stage Space Guns, Micro-Pulse Nuclear Rockets, and Faster-Than-Light Quark-Gluon Ion Drive Starships.* Blaha Research, Auburn, NH, 2013.

_____, 2013b. *Starting a Resurgent America: Solutions Destabilized America, Economy, Trade Policy, Social Security, Medicare, Obamacare, Education, Child Care, Immigration, Reviving Industry, Crime, Security, Terrorism, Prisons, Poverty, Unemployment, Media Excesses, Exporting Technology, Pollution, Waste Disposal, Space, Research, and Defense.* Pingree-Hill Publishing, Auburn, NH, 2013.

_____, *2014a. All the Multiverse! Starships Exploring the Endless Universes of the Cosmos using the Baryonic Force.* Blaha Research, Auburn, NH, 2014.

_____, *2014b. All the Multiverse! II between Multiverse Universes.* Blaha Research, Auburn, NH, 2014.

_____, 2014c. *The Rises and Falls of Man — Destiny — 3000 AD: New Support for a Superorganism MACRO-THEORY of CIVILIZATIONS From CURRENT WORLD TRENDS and NEW Peruvian, Pre-Mayan, Mayan, Anatolian, and Early Egyptian Data, with a Projection to 3000 AD* (Blaha Research, Auburn, NH, 2014).

Braudel, F. 1993. A History of Civilizations. Penguin Books. New York, NY.

Bucke, R. M. 1901. *Cosmic Consciousness* Penguin Putnam Inc., New York, 1969.

Coulborn, R. 1969. *The Origin of Civilized Societies.* Princeton University Press. Princeton, NJ.

Davies, N. 1997. *The Ancient Kingdoms of Peru.* Penguin Books. London.

Gazlake, P. S. 1973. *Great Zimbabwe.* Hazell, Watson and Viney Ltd. Alesbury, United Kingdom.

Hesiod, (Tr. H. G. Evelyn-White). 1982. *Hesiod: The Homeric Hymns and Homerica..* Harvard University Press. Cambridge, MS, USA.

Strauss, W. and Howe, N. 1991. *Generations.* William Morrow. New York.

Hodder, I. 2006. *Çatalhöyük Research Project Volume 5.* McDonald Institute Monographs/ British Institute of Archaeology at Ankara.

Hölldobler, B. and Wilson, E. O. 2009. *The Superorganism.* W.W. Norton. New York.

Huntington, S. P. 1996. *The Clash of Civilizations and the Remaking of World Order.* Simon & Schuster. New York, NY.

Iberall, A., Wilkinson, D., and White, D. 1993. *Foundations for Social and Biological Evolution.* Cri-de-Coeur Press. Laguna Hills, CA.

Kroeber, A. L. 1944. *Configurations of Culture Growth.* University of California Press. Berkeley, CA.

McGaughey, W. 2000. *Five Epochs of Civilization.* Thistlerose Publications. Milford, PA.

Mellaart, J. 1967. *Çatal Hüyük.* Thames and Hudson Ltd. London.

Moseley, M. E. 1992. *The Incas and their Ancestors.* Thames & Hudson. London.

Oppenheim, A. L. 1977. *Ancient Mesopotamia: Portrait of a Dead Civilization.* Univ. of Chicago Press. Chicago.

Pillsbury, J. 2006. *Moche Art and Archaeology in Ancient Peru.* National Gallery of Art – Studies in the History of Art. Washington DC.

Richardson, L. F. 1960. *Arms and Insecurity.* Quadrangle Books. Chicago, IL.

Roux, G. 1992. *Ancient Iraq.* Penguin Books. London.

Shklovskii, I. S., and Sagan, C. 1966. *Intelligent Life in the Universe.* Dell Publishing Co. New York, NY.

Snyder, L. D. 1999. *Macro-History – A Theoretical Approach to Comparative World History.* The Edwin Mellin Press. Lewiston, NY.

Sorokin, Pitirim. 1941. *Social and Cultural Dynamics.* four volumes. Porter Sargent Publishers. Boston, MA.

_____. 1957. *Social and Cultural Dynamics.* Abridged. Porter Sargent Publishers. Boston.

Spengler, O. 1991. *The Decline of the West.* Oxford University Press. Oxford, UK.

Sperandeo, V. 1991. *Methods of a Wall Street Master.* John Wiley & Sons. New York.

Targowski, A. 2009. *Information Technology and Societal Development.* Information Science Reference. Hersey, PA.

Toynbee, A. J. 1961. *A Study of History.* Twelve volumes. Oxford University Press. Oxford, UK, 1934-61.

Toynbee, A. J. and Somervell, D. C. 1987a. *A Study of History Abridgement of Volumes I-VI.* Oxford University Press. Oxford, UK.

_____. 1987b. *A Study of History Abridgement of Volumes VII-X.* Oxford University Press. Oxford, UK.

Wheeler, William M. 1928. *The Social Insects: Their Origin and Evolution.* Harcourt Brace. New York.

INDEX

About the Author

Stephen Blaha is an internationally known physicist with interests in Science, the Arts, and Technology. He had an Alfred P. Sloan Foundation scholarship in college. He received his Ph.D. in Physics from The Rockefeller University and has served on the faculties of several major universities. He was also a Member of the Technical Staff at Bell Laboratories, a manager at the Boston Globe Newspaper, a Director at Wang Laboratories, and President of Blaha Software Inc. and of Janus Associates Inc. (NH).

Among other achievements he was a co-discoverer of the "r potential" for heavy quark binding developing the first (and still the only demonstrable) non-abelian gauge theory with an "r" potential; first suggested the existence of topological structures in superfluid He-3; first proposed Yang-Mills theories would appear in condensed matter phenomena with non-scalar order parameters; first developed a grammar-based formalism for quantum computers and applied it to elementary particle theories; first developed a new form of quantum field theory without divergences (thus solving a major 60 year old problem that enabled a unified theory of the Standard Model and Quantum Gravity without divergences to be developed); first developed a formulation of complex Special and General Relativity based on analytic continuation from real space-time coordinates to complex coordinates; first developed a generalized non-homogeneous Robertson-Walker metric that enabled a quantum theory of the Big Bang to be developed without singularities at $t = 0$; first generalized Cauchy's theorem and Gauss' theorem to complex, curved multi-dimensional spaces; received Honorable Mention in the Gravity Research Foundation Essay Competition in 1978; first developed a physically acceptable theory of faster-than-light particles; first showed a universe with three complex spatial dimensions may be icosahedral; first derived a composition of extrema method in the Calculus of Variations; first quantitatively suggested that inflationary periods in the history of the universe were not needed; first proved Gödel's Theorem implies Nature must be quantum; first provided a new alternative to the Higgs Mechanism, and Higgs particles, to generate masses; first showed how to resolve logical paradoxes including Gödel's Undecidability Theorem by developing Operator Logic and Quantum Operator Logic; first developed a quantitative harmonic oscillator-like model of the life cycle, and interactions, of civilizations that is based on energetics (thermodynamics) with equations of the same form as those that describe superorganisms; and first developed an axiomatic derivation of the form of The Standard Model plus a Dark Particles sector from complex space-time coordinates and Asynchronous Logic. Faster than light particles are naturally a result of the Complex Lorentz group embodied in his extended Standard Model.

He has had a major impact on a succession of elementary particle theories: his Ph.D. thesis (1970), and papers, showed that quantum field theory calculations to all orders in ladder approximations could not give scaling deep inelastic electron-nucleon scattering. He later showed the eigenvalue equation for the fine structure constant α in Johnson-Baker-Willey QED had a zero at $\alpha = 1$ not 1/137 by solving the Schwinger-Dyson equations to all orders in an approximation that agreed with exact results to 8th order in α thus ending interest in this theory. In 1979 at Prof. Ken Johnson's (MIT) suggestion he calculated the proton-neutron mass difference in the MIT bag model and found the result had the wrong sign reducing interest in the bag model. These results all appear in Physical Review papers. In the 2000's he repeatedly pointed out the shortcomings of SuperString theory and showed that The Standard Model's form could be derived from space-time geometry by an extension of space-time to complex-valued coordinates, and of the Lorentz group to the complex Lorentz group (which supports faster than light transformations and particles. This deeper space-time basis shows that the Extended Standard Model developed by Blaha has an origin in geometry and is the true theory of elementary particles.

More recently Blaha has developed a theory of the Multiverse based on a complex Euclidian 16-dimensional space that explains (using the Wheeler-DeWitt equation for quantum gravity generalized to complex-valued space-times) the origin of the Cosmological Constant, the origin for the spatial asymmetry of the Universe, and an understanding of the origin of the newly found Web of Galaxies (that links all the groups of galaxies) in our universe.

He also developed proposals for faster than light starships using quark-gluon ion drives and drives based on particle-antiparticle annihilation. He designed new types of starships, uniships, which could breach the fabric of our universe and enter the multiverse with a view towards travel to other universes. As part of this development of the Multiverse he showed that a 16-dimensional baryonic field could account for the major discrepancies in experimental measurements of G, the gravitational constant. This field enables uniships to escape from our universe. In addition to uniship engine designs he described a coherent baryonic field generator that is analogous to electromagnetic lasers.

In the early 1980's Blaha was also a pioneer in the development of UNIX for financial, scientific and Internet applications: benchmarked UNIX versions showing that block size was critical for UNIX performance, developed financial modeling software, started comparative database benchmarking studies, developed Internet-like UNIX networking (1982) and developed a hybrid shell programming technique (1982) that was a precursor to the PERL programming language. He was also the database manager of the AT&T ten-year future products development database. His work helped lead to commercial UNIX on computers such as Sun Micros, IBM AIX minis, and Apple computers.

In the 1980's he pioneered the development of PC Desktop Publishing on laser printers. and was nominated for three "Awards for Technical Excellence" in 1987 by PC Magazine for PC software products that he designed and developed.

In the past twelve years Dr. Blaha has written over 40 books on a wide range of topics. Some recent major works are: *From Asynchronous Logic to The Standard Model to Superflight to the Stars*, *All the Universe!*, All the Multiverse!, and *SuperCivilizations: Civilizations as Superorganisms*.

www.ingramcontent.com/pod-product-compliance
Lightning Source LLC
Chambersburg PA
CBHW031524270326
41930CB00006B/513